Francis Close

Ritualism: a lecture, at St. James's Hall, Piccadilly

London, February 19, 1867

Francis Close

Ritualism: a lecture, at St. James's Hall, Piccadilly
London, February 19, 1867

ISBN/EAN: 9783337336370

Printed in Europe, USA, Canada, Australia, Japan

Cover: Foto ©Thomas Meinert / pixelio.de

More available books at **www.hansebooks.com**

CHURCH ASSOCIATION LECTURES.

No. II.

RITUALISM:

A LECTURE

BY

THE VERY REV. FRANCIS CLOSE, D.D.,

DEAN OF CARLISLE,

AT ST. JAMES'S HALL, PICCADILLY, LONDON,

FEBRUARY 19, 1867.

Revised by the Author.

LONDON:
WILLIAM MACINTOSH, 24, PATERNOSTER-ROW;
AND AT THE
OFFICE OF THE CHURCH ASSOCIATION,
8, ADAM-STREET, ADELPHI.

DUBLIN: G. HERBERT. LIVERPOOL: W. T. THOMPSON. BRISTOL: CHILCOTT.

1867.

RITUALISM.

THE presence of such a Meeting as this, in the midst of this busy city, and at this hour of the day, is at once a demonstration to my mind that the subject we are met to discuss is one of paramount importance. We are not here to debate whether there shall be a little more or a little less of decoration in our churches; whether we shall have a hymn or two more, or a chant or two less; nor to discuss the particular ceremonies which may be lawfully or properly introduced: but I may say for myself at least, that I come here with a deep and profound impression that we are about to explore the nature of a monstrous evil, to expose an impending danger, and to persuade each other and the world at large that if we would save the Protestant faith, and retain our open Bibles and simple worship, we must all be up and doing.

This question has made vast progress during the last eighteen months. At that time a few of us attempted, but it seemed in vain, to excite public interest upon the subject. Many were profoundly asleep upon it. They thought that these were only the strange vagaries of a few sensitive and imaginative persons, who were bent on the decoration of our churches, and the improvement of our musical worship. But the true character of that important subject which I am about to discuss, comprehended in that one single word—RITUALISM, is beginning to manifest itself. The topic can be no longer suppressed. It is evidently penetrating every grade of society, and crops out even in many pages of the public journals. Last year it was whispered in both Houses of Parliament, but I suspect that during the present session it will again be heard there, in accents long, and loud, and deep. Both Houses of Convocation debated the subject last year; and a Committee of the Lower House presented a Report to the Upper House of such a colourless character, that it has been well and sarcastically described by the Bishop of St. David's " as a *mosaic of compromises*, cemented by a general disposition in favour

A 2

of Ritualism." If this Report is to be taken as the deliberate judgment of the Lower House of Convocation, little is to be expected from them in support of the Protestant institutions of the land. But, strange to say, the Upper House, after having had a vacation to think over it, have entirely ignored this tessellated pavement of compromises, and have just passed Resolutions of the greatest importance, and calculated, in some measure, to redeem the character of the Upper House, at least in the eyes of sincere Protestants. That these Resolutions mean determination and action, I gather from the reception they met with in the Lower House. If a bombshell had burst among these clerical legislators, it could scarcely have occasioned more alarm or perturbation. They first peremptorily negatived the Bishops' Resolutions altogether: and it was only when they had denuded them of the preamble, which gave them special point against the Ritualists, that they could be got through the House. And then they were accompanied by such observations as these,—"Remember, this is not law; it is only the private opinion of the Bishops," &c. This united, unanimous declaration of the whole bench of Bishops calls for the exclamation from us, " Thank God we have a House of Lords!" I fully concur with the remarks of the celebrated S. G. O., in yesterday's *Times*, that this declaration of the Bishops must not induce us to relax our efforts against Ritualism. I would go further, and express the opinion that this important announcement of the Bishops in Convocation assembled, will be a *brutum fulmen*, or an operative agency against Ritualism, in proportion as it is or is not supported by public opinion. If you, the clergy and laity of our Church, make your convictions known and felt in all legitimate ways; and if their Lordships feel that the great majority of the Church is with them, and will support them, if necessary with pecuniary aid, rest assured the Bishops will prove true to their word.

But I now address myself to the subject before me, the great subject of RITUALISM; a topic so wide, so indefinite, so comprehensive, that it is difficult to confine myself within reasonable limits. But I will endeavour to condense my argument, and taking up Ritualism as a whole, avoid detailed branches of the subject which are properly left for discussion at subsequent lectures.

It is now well understood what we mean by RITUALISM, namely, —A GORGEOUS CEREMONIAL, VEILING THE FALSE DOCTRINES OF ROME.

I shall then endeavour to prove to this Meeting that this Ritualism is—

I. CONTRARY TO GOD'S WORD WRITTEN, BOTH HISTORICAL AND DOCTRINAL.

II. That it is opposed to the genius, the principles, and practice of the Reformed Church of England.

III. That it is a deadly peril to immortal souls.

I. In appealing to the Word of God, primarily, on the subject of a religious ceremonial, I am following the guidance of our beloved Church, who directs us to that source of Divine teaching on all subjects. And here, at the very outset, the Church of England and the Church of Rome diverge. Romanism and Ritualism always place the Church above the Bible; the Church of England always places the Bible above the Church. Not only in her Sixth Article does she teach that " Holy Scripture containeth all things necessary to salvation; so that whatsoever is not read therein, nor may be proved thereby, is not to be required of any man, that it should be believed as an article of the faith;" but throughout the whole Thirty-nine Articles, the Church assigns this as the chief reason for accepting what she believes, or rejecting anything which she disowns—namely, that it is, or is not to be found in Holy Scripture. For instance, do we accept the three Creeds as articles of the faith? Ask a Ritualist why he believes them; he will give you a long list of authorities; he will mention this Council and that Council, this saint and that saint; but what does the Church of England say? She believes them as the Eighth Article declares, "because they may be proved by most certain warrant of Holy Scripture;" not because they were held by this saint or that saint, by this man or that man. The Twenty-first Article asserts that "the Church has no power to ordain anything contrary to God's Word written; and that she is only " a witness and a keeper of Holy Writ," not a maker and sole interpreter of it! Again, she declares in her Twenty-first Article, that even " General Councils "—the highest authority that the Church on earth recognises—are not to be blindly followed; for " they may err and sometimes have erred," and are not to be believed, if what they decree is not " taken out of Holy Scripture." Again, the Church denounces " purgatory, and the invocation of saints, the adoration of images, and reliques." And why? Because they are " grounded upon no warranty of Scripture, but rather repugnant to the Word of God." She will not have her services in Latin; and why? " Because," as the Twenty-fourth Article says, "it is a thing plainly repugnant to the Word of God." Does she not believe in " Transubstantiation?" It is " because it cannot be proved by Holy Writ, but is repugnant to the plain words of Scripture." In her Article on ceremonial, the Thirty-fourth, while she admits that every Church has a right to institute its own ceremonies, she guards herself by saying, " so that

nothing be ordained against God's Word." In appealing, therefore, to Scripture, I am following in the steps of our Church ; and
it is the more necessary to do so, because certain advocates of a
gorgeous ritual are also venturing on this ground, the only ground
upon which I ever consent to meet them, the Word of God. A
distinguished person has recently come to the help of the extreme
Ritualists. They have gone down to Egypt for help—that is to
say, to America ; and they have found an American Bishop, who
has just published an elaborate work on the ceremonial of the
Christian Church, splendidly bound, with gold ornaments, which
I at first took to represent a house on fire, but afterwards found
that it was a censer with golden incense spreading its rays far
and wide. The Bishop of Vermont—Bishop Hopkins—has published this book in New York. It has not yet been published in
this country ; but it gathers importance from the fact that the
ENGLISH CHURCH UNION has circulated it widely, sending a copy
of it to each of the English bishops. I shall have occasion to refer
to it more at length as I proceed, but at present I will only remark
that the argument of Bishop Hopkins is briefly this—" The temple
worship of Israel was a gorgeous ritual : it was appointed by God
Himself ; therefore God loves a gorgeous ritual ; and if we would
serve Him most acceptably, we should adopt that ritual, as far as
we can, in the Christian Church, omitting only those rites which
are expressly prohibited." That is the Bishop's argument ; let us
examine it in the light of God's Holy Word.

Turning then to the Scriptures of Truth with this view, and
taking a rapid glance over their historical records, it appears that
for about two thousand years God was worshipped without any
ritual at all. That was the patriarchal dispensation, when men are
supposed to have walked very near to God, but totally without
Ritualistic ceremonies, incense, processions, decorations, and other
things, which we are now told are absolutely necessary. There
was then no ritual. There was the rude wayside altar, and the
atoning sacrifice ; there must be substitution, bloodshedding, death,
and burning. That was God's revealed mode of worship for two thousand years. During the two thousand years which next succeeded
in the order of time, the Mosaic dispensation was revealed by God
Himself, establishing the most elaborate ritual ever required of His
worshippers ; and here we agree with the Bishop that it was a
direct revelation from God—that every minute particular of ceremonial, down to the golden snuffers on the altar, was matter of
direct revelation from heaven,—was not only commanded by God,
but its violation was severely punished by Him. The dispensation
or ministration of Moses was emphatically a Ritualistic service, and
upon this there can be no difference of opinion.

But now we enter upon a third period of two thousand years—another and a different dispensation altogether is introduced to the world. The Son of God Himself appears and lays the foundation of the Christian religion; and according to the same inspired records, we pass insensibly from an extreme Ritualistic dispensation to one which, as far as appears on the page of Scripture, is almost as destitute of ritual as the patriarchal dispensation itself. How is this to be accounted for? Will the assumed reticence of our Divine records justify us in following the advice of the American bishop? Shall we adopt as much of the Jewish ritual as the case will allow, and shall we please God thereby? On the contrary, a slight glance at the scriptural evidence, both historical and dogmatic, will abundantly prove that the old Ritualistic dispensation was abolished and done away; and that the Christian dispensation is now established by the same Divine authority—a purer, more scriptural, more intellectual, more free, more liberal service, delivering us altogether from " the yoke of bondage " which had been a law to the Jews.

FIRST, consider our blessed Lord's own personal character and teaching. Those who are acquainted with the circumstances under which He appeared, cannot expect many open and direct declarations from Him of the abolition of the Jewish economy and ritual. The temple was still standing, and He came not to destroy, but to fulfil all the symbolic services for the justification of man. Hence His observance of the Jewish ceremonies throughout His whole life. He went up from time to time to worship at Jerusalem, and frequented the temple, and observed the holy seasons, both fasts and feasts. At the same time, it should be noticed that His chief object in frequenting the temple was to preach the Gospel. The temple was the place of public resort, like the Areopagus at Athens. There He met the assembled people, and preached day by day. The venerable Bishop of Vermont dwells much on this personal presence of Christ in the temple, arguing from it His love for ritual, and the inferential duty devolving upon us to engraft as much as possible of Jewish ritual into Christian worship, forgetting altogether the far more frequent presence of our Lord in the synagogue. The Bishop scarcely recognises this important fact, that if the Lord Jesus spent some days in the temple, He spent many more in the synagogue. There He taught and preached Sabbath after Sabbath; and the synagogue worship far more resembles our Christian worship than did the temple worship. And there are those outside this controversy who have shown much learning in proving that our Evangelical worship is an imitation rather of the synagogue worship than of the temple worship. But the Bishop's argument falls to the ground; for if, as he argues, we ought to imitate the temple worship because Christ frequented it, we must, on the same grounds, imitate the synagogue worship because He frequented that still more frequently.

Turning to another subject, we have a remarkable evidence of the simple character of the Christian ministration and worship in the fulfilment of a well-known prophecy—that the glory of the second temple should exceed that of the first. The glory of the first temple consisted not only in the splendour of the building itself and its costly architecture, but in the visible presence of God Himself. At its dedication the majesty of Jehovah was so awfully displayed that the priests fled out of the temple from the greatness of that glory. How was the second temple to exceed the first in glory? Not in its architecture, not in the richness of its decorations, certainly not in its visible glory. But all are agreed that the glory of the second temple consisted in the presence of God manifest in the flesh. Now how did God manifest in the flesh appear? As a poor, simple, unadorned man, " in whom there was no beauty that they should desire him," with no train of angels, no glory round His head. There was the spiritual founder of the Christian religion, destitute of outward pomp and show; yet He said of Himself, " That in this place is one greater than the temple."

On several occasions in the course of His ministry our blessed Lord dropped into the ear of favoured individuals intimations of what was to come to pass; as in that well-known passage in St. John (iv. 21—24), when He assured the Samaritan woman that all Ritual distinctions were about to be done away ; and that " the hour cometh when ye shall neither in this mountain, nor yet at Jerusalem, worship the Father. The hour cometh and now is when the true worshippers shall worship the Father in spirit and in truth," anywhere and everywhere alike. So, when describing His Gospel kingdom to His disciples, He said, " The kingdom of God cometh not with observation," or, as it is in the margin, " with outward show."* Ritualism, on the contrary, is all display, there is nothing to be done without a full train of monks, and processions, with which they tell us St. Augustine converted England.

Again, on a certain occasion, when the Saviour was retiring from the Temple where He had been labouring all day long, one of His disciples pointed out to Him the beautiful stones of the Temple, and said, " Master, see what manner of stones and what buildings are here!" He said, " Seest thou these great buildings? there shall not be left one stone upon another, that shall not be thrown down."† Portentous and comprehensive prophecy ! Not

---

* Luke xvii. 20.   † Mark xiii. 1, 2.

merely shall Jerusalem be destroyed and the Jewish polity swept away, but the whole symbolic system of temple worship along with it! Its altar, its sacrifices, its priests and Levites—all shall come to an end! so that God's people should not be able to offer a sacrifice if they would!

Regard for a moment the institution of that only ordinance which our Lord appointed before He suffered. What marked simplicity, what a total absence of ceremony! It was after the Passover. It was therefore after a full meal: for the Jews were obliged to consume the whole lamb at the Passover. It was in the evening, not in the morning, "the very night in which He was betrayed," destitute of all show and decoration. It is hardly possible to conceive anything so dissimilar as the original institution of the Lord's Supper and the Romish mass, or the Ritualistic "eucharistic sacrifice." It would seem that they really went out òf their way to make their gaudy worship as little like the Holy Supper as possible. It was instituted in the *evening*, and they say that it ought to be taken in the *morning :* it was received after a full meal, they take it fasting : they change the bread into a wafer, and mingle water with the wine! So that hardly a trace of the original institution is to be discovered in their elaborate service.

But another event of a most startling and miraculous description demands our attention. Among the wonders of Mount Calvary, as the Lord Jesus hung upon the cross, when He bowed His head and gave up the ghost, the veil of the Temple which had concealed the most Holy Place for a thousand years—that veil whose mysteries even a pious priest would sooner die than attempt to penetrate—was by some invisible hand rent in twain from the top to the bottom! It was at the hour of evening prayer, when probably unusual multitudes were assembled because of the miraculous darkness, when this strange event occurred—laying bare to the gaze of the wondering priests, who would tell the sign to the astonished people, the place where God was. Is it possible to conceive any supernatural portent more calculated to convey the truth, that the system of symbolism, mystery, and ritual was about to be for ever abolished ?

After His death and resurrection our Lord never again visited the Temple. He had done with its forms and symbols—and that dispensation had passed away! In His intercourse with His disciples He entered into spiritual subjects, but He gave them no instructions relative to the mode of religious worship. He bade them go "into all the world and preach the Gospel," "baptizing," but He prescribed no form, only they were to use water "in the name of the Father, and of the Son, and of the Holy Ghost." How much water was to be used, or whether persons were to be immersed, or washed, or sprinkled, He did not decide; neither form nor ceremony was commanded. He laid down great principles, and gave them the simplest conceivable ordinance: This is the Christian religion, this is the mind of Christ on Ritual!

Hence arises one of the most forcible negative arguments against extreme Ritual in the Christian Church. From the time when the disciples saw the Lord go up into heaven to the latest date of the Scripture narrative not a trace is to be found of a gorgeous Ritual! If any had existed it is quite impossible but that in some of the narratives it must have appeared. But not a vestige is to be found except it be hidden in St. Paul's cloak that he left behind him at Troas! In default of any rational evidence, the high Ritualists, following some old wives' fable of the dark ages, have fixed on this cloak, as some religious dress, a cope or some monkish attire! Outside commentators have innocently imagined that it was part of the ordinary Roman dress: but this is too common, perhaps an Erastian view of the subject! Might it not be suggested to these Ritualistic archæologists that this cloak may be the identical mantle which fell from the shoulders of Elijah on Elisha? There are many things in Ritualism and Romanism not less absurd than this suggestion.

Who would conceive it possible that the Ritualists could press another story into their service? It is mentioned that there were many lights in the upper chamber where Paul was long preaching, and they conclude that those lights must have been the decorations of an high altar! It does not occur to them, that being midnight it was dark at the time, and that candles were lighted for the purpose of enabling people to see—just the reverse of their practice. They light candles on their altar in broad daylight, and in the face of the glorious sun! emblematic it may be of the paltry light of Ritualism, as contrasted with the Gospel of Christ. But enough of these feeble suggestions. Throughout the whole of the sacred story, no encouragement is afforded, no indication whatever is given, that any part or portion of the Mosaic Ritual was to be engrafted into the Christian Church. On the contrary, further investigation will prove that there are strong evidences to the contrary, and not a few direct testimonies against it.

Bishop Hopkins dwells much on the fact that, immediately after the Day of Pentecost, and some years subsequently, the Apostles and the early Christians observed various Jewish ceremonies, attended the Temple, and recognised the appointed fasts and feasts; and he mentions that St. Paul himself, in deference to the High Church party, at Jerusalem, "those of the circumcision," observed some Jewish rites, entered into the

Temple, " and shaved his head ; " a compromise which did not seem to be followed up with a providential blessing, but involved disastrous consequences, was the occasion of his imprisonment, and reversed the policy of James, who advised this course to please the many Jews who believed. But the Bishop forgets that the Church was in its infancy at that time, that it was then exclusively Jewish. No Gentile was yet called ; that mystery had not yet been revealed. It was on the calling of the Gentiles that St. Peter first spoke . out boldly in favour of the liberty of the Christian Church. Returning from his mission. to Cornelius, he was violently opposed by the more bigoted Christian Jews, who rebuked him for going among the Gentiles. Peter on this occasion assumed no authority, nor did he claim the power of the keys. He was compelled to produce arguments, and facts, and witnesses to prove that this was God's doing; and it was then only that the opposers yielded, saying, " that unto the Gentiles also God hath granted repentance unto life." On a subsequent occasion the same Apostle of the circumcision, in pleading this cause, used these remarkable words,—" Why tempt ye God, to put a yoke upon the neck of the disciples, which neither our fathers nor we were able to bear ? "* Moreover, we have direct evidence respecting this same Peter, that he himself abandoned Jewish customs, " and lived as did the Gentiles." Paul withstood Peter to his face. And why ? Because he said, before the Jews of the circumcision came to Antioch, " You, Peter, lived as do the Gentiles." He had abandoned the Jewish practices altogether as a man ought to do who belonged to a Church in which there is no difference between the " Jew and the Greek." But no sooner did James and his party come down from Jerusalem than he separated himself from the Gentiles, and became a Jew again ; and it was for this that Paul withstood him to his face (Gal. ii. 11—15), proving not only the freedom of the Gentiles from Jewish rites, but the departure of Christian Jews from their Mosaic Ritual. Throughout the Epistle to the Galatians St. Paul argues this blessed truth. In chapter iv. 9, he says, " Now, after that ye have known God, how turn ye again *to the weak and beggarly elements ?* " What were they ? The very ceremonies which God himself had appointed! Here is an answer to the Bishop. They were ceremonies for the time ; Divine ordinances, but no longer in force; done away in Christ! " How turn ye again to the *weak and beggarly elements,* whereunto ye desire again to be in *bondage ?* Ye observe days, and months, and times, and years. I am afraid of you." And after much such reasoning, he adds,—" Stand fast, therefore, in the liberty wherewith Christ hath

* Acts xv. 10.

made us free, and be not entangled again with *the yoke of bondage.*"
There is another magnificent passage to the same effect in 2 Cor.
iii. 7—11. I can only glance at it. There St. Paul is contrasting the
old dispensation with the new. One he calls "the ministration of death," the other "the ministration of the Spirit;"
one "the ministration of condemnation," the other "the ministration of righteousness." He admits that there had been a
glory in the Jewish dispensation; but he says, "If the ministry
of condemnation be glory, much more doth the ministration of
righteousness exceed in glory. For even that which was made
glorious had no glory in this respect by reason of the glory that
excelleth. For if that which was done away was glorious, much
more that which remaineth is glorious." And this is the doctrine
of the Apostle throughout his epistles. The dispensation of Moses
was, from its very nature, its symbolical character, doomed to pass
away. When the thing symbolized appeared, when the Saviour
came, when the one great sacrifice was offered, when everything
was "finished" which God desired in order to reconcile man to
himself,—away with the symbols: we no longer need the outward
figures when that which was the object of those figures is fully ac-
complished.

Other passages of Scripture, bearing the same import, multiply
upon us; and though fearing to exhaust your patience, I must
refer to some of them, the result of my own earnest search into
God's Word on this important subject—the fallacies of Ritualism.
Thus in the Epistle to the Colossians (ii. 13—19, 21, 22) the distinctive feature of the Jewish ceremonial is clearly defined—it was
a *shadow*, not the *substance* :—"Let no man therefore judge you
in meat, or in drink, or in respect of a holiday, or of the new moon,
or of the Sabbath-days; which are a *shadow* of things to come;
but the *body* is of *Christ.*" There is the substance,—"Let no man
beguile you of your reward in a voluntary humility, and worshipping of angels, intruding into those things which he hath not seen,
vainly puffed up in his fleshly mind. And not holding the head,
from which all the body by joints and bands having nourishment
ministered, and knit together increaseth with the increase of God.
Wherefore if ye be dead with Christ from the rudiments of the world"
—intending the carnal ordinances of Moses—"why as though
living in the world, are ye subject to ordinances—(touch not, taste
not, handle not; which all are to perish with the using)—after the
commandments and doctrines of men; which things have indeed a
show of wisdom in will worship, and humility, and neglecting of
the body : not in any honour to the satisfying of the flesh." That
is the Apostle's clear protest against the introduction of Jewish
Ritualism into the Christian Church.

The Epistle of St. Paul to the Hebrews, as a whole, from the beginning to the end, is one grand testimony to the finished work of Christ, the accomplishment of prophecy, the realization of symbolic worship in Christ, and our entire deliverance from the bondage of minute Ritualistic and legal worship. " Now of the things which we have spoken," saith he (chap. viii. 1, 2), " this is the sum: we have such an high priest, who is set on the right hand of the throne of the majesty in the heavens; a minister of the sanctuary, and of the true tabernacle, which the Lord pitched, and not man." And in the ninth chapter the Apostle, reviewing all those " carnal ordinances " of Jewish worship which excite the admiration of Bishop Hopkins, and which he would reproduce in the Christian Church, declared that they only " signified that the way to the holiest of all was not yet manifest, while as the first tabernacle was yet standing : *which was a figure for the time then present* "..... "which stood only in meats and drinks, and divers washings, and carnal ordinances, *imposed on them until the time of Reformation.* BUT CHRIST BEING COME,"—he proceeds to establish the Gospel system on the ruins of Judaism ! and he leads on those to whom he wrote to that sublime consummation of spiritual, heavenly worship, contrasting gloriously with the visible, histrionic worship of modern Ritual :—" Ye are not come unto the mount that might be touched, and that burned with fire, nor unto blackness, and darkness, and tempest, and the sound of a trumpet, and the voice of words; which voice they that heard intreated that the word should not be spoken to them any more. But ye are come unto Mount Sion, and unto the city of the living God, the heavenly Jerusalem, and to an innumerable company of angels, to the general assembly and church of the firstborn, which are written in heaven, and to God the Judge of all, and to the spirits of just men made perfect. And to Jesus, the mediator of the New Covenant." " Wherefore," he saith, " we, receiving a kingdom which cannot be moved, let us have grace whereby we may serve God acceptably with reverence and godly fear." What more do we need ? We have a reconciled God and friend in Christ Jesus; the way is open to us. " Let us come boldly unto the throne of grace," not crawling, prostrate, and kissing the floor, as some Ritualists have taught even ladies to come,—postures worthy only of the worship of the horrible gods of the heathen, but utterly unbecoming in a Christian, " whose body is the temple of the Holy Ghost."

But let it be remembered that when I speak of Ritualists, I do not designate as such those who may have merely indulged in a little more decoration of their services; but I speak of the fullblown, fully developed Ritualism, of " *The Church and the*

World,"—such as is displayed in those innumerable controversial and devotional tracts circulated widely in their congregations, and bearing on their face the most unblushing Popery. Here may be found the hopeless and desperate attempt to justify their gaudy worship by an appeal to the Book of Revelation. It could hardly be believed than even a Ritualist would claim the heavenly visions of St. John as authority for introducing histrionic services into the Christian worship. The attempt is so puerile, so simple, that if it were not gravely propounded it would be beneath notice! Is it so that they have not a poet or a prophet among them, some one accustomed to the wild imagery of Scripture, who might persuade them that the visions of St. John were not intended to convey a material representation of scenes in the heavenly worship, but by a region of imagery to awaken holy and lofty anticipations in our minds? Or, if they will persist in copying the imaginary pictures of heavenly worship, let them copy them faithfully, put foot-lights to their histrionic stage, and introduce all the monsters of the vision, with eyes all over them, or with human heads and bodies of animals. The thought is profane, revolting! Such actings and such arguments offend our common sense. They chill our blood, and we become ashamed of an age which we thought was called advanced. We are driven back by such senseless reasoning to the dark ages!

Now it is in support of such vain traditions as these that the Bishop of Vermont, in the United States, appears as an advocate. His work* would hardly call for so much notice had it not been adopted by the ENGLISH CHURCH UNION, and distributed by them among the English bishops. He lays it down as a primary dogma "that the Divine and only model of all ritual worship is in the tabernacle and temple (of the Jews),—priestly vestments, embroidery, precious stones, incense, anointing oils, the golden candlestick, choral service in the temple, and all this by Divine command," these are models equally for Christian worship. Not only so,—our episcopal guide furnishes us with an enumeration of various articles and ceremonies which he affirms were adopted by the *Primitive Church.*

Now by the Primitive Church we used to understand the Church of the Apostles, for the first sixty or one hundred years of Christianity. But the Ritualistic Primitive Church is the Church at the close of the third and the beginning of the fourth century. It was primitive in one sense, for it was the beginning of all darkness and superstition. The Bishop tells us that these are the " points of voluntary conformity to the Mosaic ritual on the part of the

* " The Law of Ritualism."—Hurd, New York.

Primitive Church :—Orientation, position of the altar, the atrium, gates and veils, separation of sexes, texts, altars, legs, stone altars, candles or lamps, incense, bowing towards the altar, chrism in confirmation, vestments, sticharia and tunicles, orarium, alb, dalmatic." Now such a list as this would have puzzled St. Paul himself. They are hard words which were not known in the Primitive Church. They were discovered ages afterwards, and yet a Protestant Bishop assures us that these things were adopted in the Primitive Church. This is worthy of a bishop who for fifty years has been the advocate of American slavery. But we will do him justice. Bishop Hopkins is a good Protestant after all. The influence of old mother Church has not quite been lost on him. He allows that if what he finds in the Jewish ritual ought to be in the Christian ritual, that which he does not find in the Jewish ritual ought not to be in the Christian ritual. Upon this principle the Bishop abjures six or eight of the Roman doctrines which are espoused by the English Ritualists. He is a gorgeous Ritualist, but no Papist, and therefore ought not to be quoted as an advocate for modern English Ritualism. " Things not in Israel, and therefore not in the Christian Church. 1. No Pope. 2. No saint worship. 3. No priestly celibacy. 4. No auricular confession. 5. No purgatory. 6. No monasticism. 7. No adding of new articles of faith." Now here is a bishop, who is put forward by the English Church Union as their advocate for a gorgeous ritual, positively denying five of their grand fundamental principles on which they found their ritual. Here is this Republican bishop making a raid on all these favourite doctrines. What! No Pope, no celibacy, no purgatory, and, above all, no auricular confession? What can Dr. Pusey and his friends say but " Ye have taken away my gods, and what have I more ? "

But I have not done with the English Church Union. Observe their inconsistency. Here is a book imported from America, splendidly bound, and sent to all our bishops by the English Church Union. Of course you will suppose they authenticated it —that they take the Bishop as their advocate for gorgeous Ritualism.

But how is this, when their episcopal advocate denies several of their chief doctrines? Is it that they may exhibit this book to a casual reader, and leave him to conclude that they agree with Bishop Hopkins in repudiating these tenets, and that Ritualists in general repudiate them? The circulation of this book by the English Church Union is in every way a disingenuous act. They invade Cumberland and other places, and deny that the English Church Union is Ritualistic! Why, then, do they circulate this book, which is a laboured defence of a gorgeous ritual ? Or being Ritualists, in the English sense, how can they circulate a work which cuts from under them the very dogmas on which they themselves build their Ritualism? Leaving them to the choice of these dilemmas, I record my conviction that the English Church Union is one of the most formidable instruments for promoting that reign of Popish darkness with which Ritualism threatens us. And that this is no peculiar conviction of mine, is evident from the fact, that two of their most distinguished members and office-bearers have publicly seceded from the Union on this very consideration. Professor M. Burrows, Chairman of their Oxford Branch, avowedly left them in consequence of the Ritualistic measures adopted at head-quarters; and the Rev. Dr. Jebb, Chairman of the Hereford Branch, who is anything but an anti-Ritualist, secedes, on account of the adoption of Dr. Pusey's "Eirenicon." These are edifying examples, and may induce many other moderate Churchmen who have joined the Union, without sufficiently examining their true principles, in like manner to secede from them. An Institution which receives the adhesion of Dr. Pusey with acclamation, and from which such influential, wise, and moderate men as Professor M. Burrows and Dr. Jebb retire, carries with it its own condemnation.

Having designedly occupied so much time in the investigation of the Scriptural argument against Ritualism in the Christian Church, and having also met the statements of our opponents on that ground, my remarks on the second part of my subject must be very brief. And they need not be otherwise, for it must already be self-evident THAT RITUALISM IS OPPOSED TO THE USAGE, GENIUS, AND PRINCIPLES OF THE REFORMED CHURCH ESTABLISHED IN THIS LAND. I shall, therefore, content myself with briefly appealing to honest common sense, to undoubted facts, and to the testimony of one or two witnesses whose evidence cannot easily be set aside. The Bishop of St. David's learned, philosophic, and weighty charge is almost exhaustive on this subject; and an admirable article in the last " Quarterly Review " places the state of the legal question most clearly before us.

But turning to the broad facts of the case, we may ask, if this gorgeous ritual was not contrary to the principles of our Reformed Church, why was it ever abolished? What in the name of common sense drove all this Ritualism out of the Church of England, if it always properly belonged to it? Have we, like the people in the " Arabian Nights," been asleep and turned into stone for the last three hundred yeras, and must we turn back again to what we were three hundred years ago? The idea of a party in the Church calling upon us to do so, is the most preposterous suggestion that was ever made.

Again, the identity of Ritualism with the principles and practices, and ceremonies and dogmas of the Church of Rome at once proves that it is contrary to the principles of the Church of England. Why did the Church of England secede from the Church of Rome? Because she wanted to shake hands with the Church of Rome as Dr. Pusey does? No; but because she believed, and made people in Parliament swear they believed, her doctrines to be damnable. Has Popery changed? Have we changed? No. How, then, can we retain in the bosom of our Reformed Church the Ritualists who have been convicted over and over again of being Romanists, both in practice and principle? Why should we allow them to remain in our Church, and fraternize with them?

In the celebrated Report of the Committee of the Lower House of Convocation it is stated, with regard to Ritualism, " In the larger number of cases we can see no proper connexion with the distinctive teaching of the Church of Rome." Now none are so blind as those who will not see. The Bishop of St. David's stands aghast, and says he cannot comprehend how men can shut their eyes so as to deny the direct Romish tendency of these proceedings. And he expresses more astonishment when he hears one high in office and position say " that this present movement is not a movement towards Rome." If so, I ask, Whither does it lead us? If this is not the road towards Rome, I don't know any other road so direct towards it. The Bishop of St. David's indignantly writes thus:—" Nothing, in my judgment, can be more mischievous, as well as in more direct contradiction to notorious facts, than to deny or ignore the Romeward tendency of the movement." Again, I say, thank God that we have bishops who will speak out plainly. But the Bishop further exposes the practice of these men. There is no question whatever that in the Ritualism which appears in public we see not one half of what is going on, and that the hidden Ritualism is more dangerous than the open Ritualism; and that Ritualism the Bishop calls the " adulteration " of the Church of England services. Ritualistic priests circulate books of devotion which are to be read by the devout while the Communion is going on, their " eucharistic sacrifice." These books are taken verbatim from the religious books of Rome. They are in some respects worse than Rome, inculcating the profoundest homage towards that which they assert is present in the consecrated elements, whatever that may be. The Bishop of St. David's speaks of these attempts with indignation. Alluding to their attempts to bring our Communion office into harmony with the Mass, he says, " I must own that there is something in the adulteration—as I think I may not improperly call it—of the Prayer-book out of the Missal, which, to my sense, has an unpleasant savour

of artifice and disingenuousness. It is a proceeding of which I
think both Churches have reason to complain; the one, that her
mind is not only disregarded, but misrepresented; the other, that
her treasures are rifled to set off her adversary with a false resem-
blance of likeness to herself."

But I proceed to my last point, and that which presses most
deeply upon my heart. Its importance cannot be overrated. The
painful study of writers of this school during the last eighteen months
has deeply impressed me with the conviction THAT THE WHOLE
SYSTEM OF RITUALISM IS DESTRUCTIVE OF IMMORTAL SOULS, THAT
IT IS AN OBSCURATION OF GOD'S TRUTH, AN ADULTERATION OF
CHRIST'S GOSPEL, AND IS PERILOUS TO THE SALVATION OF EVERY
ONE WHO COMES WITHIN ITS INFLUENCE! I have imbibed this
conviction from the following considerations:—1. *Ritualism is
dangerous and perilous to the soul, because it is a system of sensu-
ousness.* It is built upon a false foundation; it rests only or
chiefly on the feelings, affections, and imaginations and nervous
system of the natural man. Ritualism, in its highest and deepest
character, manifestly operates on that which is visible, earthly, and
carnal. It is a religion of sight, not of faith. It dazzles the
eyes with the splendour of its altars and its gaudy shows; it
pleases the ear with melodious sounds; even the olfactory nerves
are soothed by its incense. It bewitches the morbid senses of
men, and, most of all, of women; and, soothed, and charmed, and
flattered by that which is all sensuous and carnal, its deluded
servants fancy they are religious!

Many years ago a sceptical physician said to me:—"I never
felt religious but once in my life." "When was that?" I inquired.
His reply was, "When I was gazing on Stonehenge by moonlight!" "Then," said I, "depend upon it, you never felt
religious at all in your life! That was not religion. It was
the natural superstition of the fallen human heart awakened by
the romance of moonlight, and ruins, and sensuous impressions,
which may be aroused by the picturesque and beautiful, whether
in heathen or Ritualistic worship." "The natural man receiveth
not the things of the Spirit of God; for they are foolishness unto
him." And he substitutes for them something that he can see,
and hear, and smell, and touch! The spiritual man "discerneth
things spiritual," endures as seeing him who "is invisible;"
needs not, but rejects pictures and carved images either of holy
persons or dogmas; worships the invisible Spirit; and by faith
contemplates Him "whom having not seen we love: in whom
though now we see him not"—pictured and sculptured—"yet
believing, we rejoice with joy unspeakable and full of glory."
"*Faith* is the *substance* of things hoped for, the evidence of things

not seen as yet." "For the things which are seen are temporal, but the things which are not seen are eternal." Spiritual religion is opposed to a religion of sound, and sense, and merely natural feeling. Gracious was the word of the Lord to Thomas whose wavering faith the Saviour strengthened and restored :—"Thomas, because thou hast seen me thou hast believed"—that is an inferior faith—"but *blessed are they that have not seen and yet have believed.*"

2. RITUALISM *is not only* A SENSUOUS RELIGION, BUT ONE THAT "ENGENDERETH BONDAGE." It is hardly possible to read the religious books to which I have referred without smiling at the whimsical and extraordinary instructions given by these priests to the people. They are told how to come into church, and how to go out of church, how they are to cross their hands and bend their knees, and to do this, and that, and the other. Why, it is bondage. It is like the bondage of the Pharisees who laid burdens on other men, and would not touch them with their own fingers. It is the burden of the Jewish system. And it is monstrous that one man, let him call himself parson, priest, or deacon, should lay down rules for another man as to what he is to eat and to drink, and the penance he is to perform. It is the bondage which Popery has laid upon the world for centuries, and which these semi-Papists would again impose upon us.

3. *Ritualism is perilous to the soul because it is essentially Romanism,* and every doctrine properly Roman or Popish is perilous to the soul. Can I believe in many mediators without dishonouring the Great Mediator? Can I believe that the heart of Mary is more tender than the heart of her Son, without impugning the love of Him "who is touched with the feeling of my infirmities?" Shall I go to a priest, a sinner like myself, to be absolved from my sins, when my Saviour has absolved me already? Shall I ask Peter, or John, or the Virgin Mary to pray for me, when I have already "an advocate with the Father, Christ the righteous?" Shall I go to the servant, when I have the ear of the Son? Away with such useless friends, such inferior mediators and deities—"miserable comforters are ye all!"

Take what doctrines of Romanism and Ritualism you may, they are equally destructive of souls. Purgatory, Auricular Confession! That above all tends to delude the soul with false peace. Every-one knows that no tenet of Rome has occasioned more scandal or created more immorality than this; the greatest abuses and abominations have flowed from it. But apart from these, let Auricular Confession be conducted in the purest and most skilful manner, it is still a fraud and a delusion on the soul—and above all else brings it into bondage. The confessor may put the seal

of confession on his lips, but the poor dupe is now in his power—
the secrets of his or her heart are known to a fellow-sinner, and
who can calculate the moral tyranny which must follow ?

But these unscriptural and perilous doctrines will be taken up
in detail by lecturers who will succeed me. I will therefore only
assert, generally, that the false dogmas of Rome, with which
Ritualism has "adulterated" the services of our Church, are
perilous to the soul and dishonouring to Christ, whom Ritualists
profess to magnify in their meretricious ceremonies.

4. *Ritualism is perilous to the soul because it sets up fallacious and
false standards of casuistry*—bewildering men's consciences, and
confounding the principles of right and wrong. Cases of this
description might be easily multiplied—and the charge is
abundantly established against sundry Ritualistic authors, by the
writer in the last "Quarterly Review," to whom I have before
referred. And here I know I enter upon delicate and difficult
ground : but if Paul withstood Peter to the face, because the great
apostle of the circumcision erred in a very similar manner, I will
not shrink from freely expressing my opinion upon a transaction
of a public nature affecting the moral judgment of one highly
respected.

I thank God that although I am a controversialist of forty
years' standing, I have never been accused of speaking evil of the
private character of any one. But public men and public acts are
the subject of public judgment. An event has recently occurred
in the Church which is calculated to show how the mysticism of a
false casuistry may so entangle and beguile the mind of a good man
that he may put darkness for light and light for darkness. Most
persons are aware of what has occurred respecting a hymn of the
late Mr. Keble, where the expression is used, " Christ in the heart,
not in the hand." In thousands and tens of thousands of Protestant
minds that hymn was a comfortable assurance that its author meant
that the real objective presence of Christ was not in the hand ; that
Christ was in the heart alone, and not in the bread in their hands.
This is the sense in which it was universally understood. But Mr.
Keble's friends were very anxious to alter these words, and to alter
them in a way which to a plain Protestant reader destroyed their
original meaning—" Christ in the heart *and* in the hand." The
matter was debated, and it was determined that the alteration should
take place with the consent of Mr. Keble. It is not for the purpose of censuring Mr. Keble that I refer to this, but to call
attention to the casuistry of Dr. Pusey on the subject. Dr. Pusey
stands over the grave of his friend, and appears as an apologist for
the words originally used, and for this alteration. It appears that
Mr. Keble's explanation of this to himself was that the words "not

in the hand" did not mean what people generally thought—that they only suggested that it was not sufficient to have Christ in the hand, but that He must also be in the heart. "This," says Dr. Pusey, "is plainly not the obvious meaning of the words, but it satisfied him," and it satisfied Dr. Pusey. The Reviewer observes on this transaction:—"Thus it would seem that, according to his most intimate friend, Mr. Keble was, for perhaps thirty years, in the habit of explaining his own words to himself in an unnatural sense, while he allowed them to go forth in hundreds of thousands of copies with the knowledge that to all readers they would carry that obvious meaning which he had originally taken from Hooker, and which is alone consistent with the original drift of the poem." *

Upon this strange event I would make only one remark. While I am fully persuaded that Dr. Pusey does not intend to sanction anything wrong, evasive, or untrue, a man who can make such an apology for such a course of conduct, and does not see that the apology is worse than the fact itself, must have a moral mist over his mind, and must be misled by an erroneous casuistry.

Neither can plain and ordinary moralists comprehend the process by which so eminent a divine can justify his attempt to reconcile and harmonize the Decrees of the Council of Trent with the Thirty-nine Articles of the Church of England. It is strange indeed! To unite darkness and light, truth and error, or any thing which can be more opposite to any other thing, would be a task more simple, more straightforward. It is evident that the Bishop of St. Davids, in his Charge, is equally perplexed, and points his energetic reasoning to expose the sophistry by which such an attempt is supported. One can only fear that the Professor, having been, as he tells us, for thirty years occupied in receiving confessions, and dealing with the subtlest cases of casuistry, has lost a clear perception of simple truth and error.

I confess to a little satisfaction when I read in the public journals the announcement that Dr. Pusey's "Eirenicon" and "Ecce Homo," the representatives of the two evils which at present distract our Church, were, by the same decree of the HOLY COLLEGE at ROME, placed in the "*Index Expurgatorius*," and publicly denounced as dangerous and forbidden books, not to be read by any good Catholics! This does seem somewhat ungenerous in the Head of the Roman Church, since Dr. Pusey has in this very work sacrificed nearly all the peculiar tenets of the Reformed Church in his sanguine but vain attempt to reconcile us with Rome.†

* "Quarterly Review," No. 243, January, 1867, p. 202.
† Extract from "A Second Letter on the Present Position of the High Church

For once I agree with the Pope, believing and knowing well that no compromise will satisfy him ; nor can any union take place between the Reformed Churches and Rome, except on the terms of unconditional surrender of all our principles to that arbitrary and unscriptural Power.

With the casuistry and moral teaching of many of the less distinguished writers and priests of this Ritualistic school one can hardly deal so tenderly. In too many of their publications, as I can attest myself, the observation of the Quarterly Reviewer is fearfully exemplified—"*the commonest sense of the duty of truth-fulness is palpably wanting.*"* And what shall we say to a priest of the Catholic revival school who, having been in the habit of turning his back on the congregation, and elevating his wheaten deity above his head for the adoration of the faithful, discovers that this is an act clearly illegal in our Reformed Church of England ; so he abandons the practice, but at the same time suggests to his congregation that in consecrating the elements on the north side of what he calls his "altar," he can so exhibit them that the people may still ADORE! This may be observing the law in the letter, but grossly violating it in the spirit! In older and more plain-speaking times this would have been called "A PIOUS FRAUD." It is impossible that the legal quirks and quibbles by which a Popish ritual is dovetailed with our honest Reformed services can be supported with such ingenious sophistries, without corrupt-ing the moral sense of the people; and I fully concur in the severe remarks of the reviewer—" Even if the new movement should gain a strong hold on the shopkeeping class, we cannot bring ourselves to regard that event as an unmixed benefit to society ; for what confidence could we have in the weights and measures, or the assurances of tradesmen who should have been infused with the casuistical principles of the school with which we have been

Party in the Church of England," by the Rev. Wm. Maskell, Vicar of St. Mary's Church. Third Edition. London : Pickering. 1850. Pp. 64, 65, note :—
    "I have heard both clergy and laity of the Church of England—and that within the last twelve months—declare that they accept and believe all Christian truth, as it is explained in the Decrees and Canons of the Council of Trent. With regard to such a statement by any of our laity, it is curious, to say the least of it, and probably was never made by one who had read or understood the Tridentine Canons. But, as to clergymen, ignorance cannot be supposed ; and for them, bound as they are by subscription to our formularies, thus to speak, has always seemed to me amongst the greatest of all achievements of the human intellect. Subtle as we know the mind of man to be, and wide its range, I cannot but confess that the more I think of it, the more I am amazed at so won-derful an example of its power and capability. There are not perhaps many minds so large ; I cannot tell. But there have not been many Homers, Platos, or Isaac Newtons."
    * "Quarterly," p. 205.

dealing ? " This is an obvious and inevitable conclusion. If the Bishop of St. David's has proved that the teachers and the priests will adulterate the Church service, surely one taught by them will think it no great harm to adulterate the tea or sugar in which he deals. In truth this is no new charge, no uncertain theory. Those who are acquainted with the secrets of the Romish confessional, with its arbitrary distinctions of mortal sins, its venial sins, its great sins and little sins, and the dangerous refinements of its whole moral code, know that it is a system destructive of all plain straight-forward honesty which is the glory of England. Ritualism has adopted the vicious system of the Roman discipline, and the consequences are unavoidable. I solemnly warn you against it, because it is opposed to God's Word written,—because it is opposed to the genius and principles of the Reformed Church of England and of all reformed Churches,—and because it is perilous to immortal souls, training them up in a casuistry which is unnatural, false, and sophistical.

Let us then offer it every opposition in our power. There has been considerable debating amongst us as to the manner in which it should be resisted. Some persons are in favour of an application to Parliament, some are for legal proceedings, and some would look to the bishops. Our divided counsels have afforded encouragement to our adversaries,—but without reason. My advice is, attack them at all points and by all means. It is not necessary that one only method should be pursued, nor can we say which will succeed, this or that; only let us contend for the customs and liberties of three hundred years, protesting against this subtle revival of Popery, for it is nothing less. The class most formidable to the Ritualists is the churchwardens, and if those useful and important Church officers throughout the country were staunch to the principles and practices of the Reformation, they might legally restrain the Ritualistic clergy in their Romish practices, and do more than any other persons effectually to put them down. Knowing this, Ritualists generally contrive to get their disciples into this office.

Brother members of " that pure and reformed part of the holy Catholic Church established in this land," let us adopt any and all measures which are legitimate, honest, open, courageous, for the suppression of this gaudy Ritualism, this meretricious Romanism !

CHURCH ASSOCIATION LECTURES.

No. I.

PRIESTHOOD:

A LECTURE

BY

THE REV. HUGH M'NEILE, D.D.,

CANON OF CHESTER,

AT ST. JAMES'S HALL, PICCADILLY, LONDON,

ON TUESDAY, FEBRUARY 12, 1867.

Revised by the Author.

LONDON:

WILLIAM MACINTOSH, 24, PATERNOSTER-ROW;

AND AT THE

OFFICE OF THE CHURCH ASSOCIATION,

8, ADAM-STREET, ADELPHI.

DUBLIN: G. HERBERT. LIVERPOOL: W. T. THOMPSON. BRISTOL: CHILCOTT.

1867.

PRIESTHOOD.

THERE is a retribution in Divine Providence, and duty cannot be neglected with eventual impunity. It is not too much to say that the present state of our national Church, as a house divided against itself, is retributive for duty neglected somewhere. I do not say where; probably in more directions than one. We make no pretence to infallibility of judgment, or to absolute blamelessness of conduct, and therefore we willingly accept our share of the verdict of neglect for time past, whilst we humbly pray our heavenly Father that for the time to come we may perceive and know what things we ought to do, and also have grace and power faithfully to fulfil the same.

In complying with the request of the Committee of the Church Association to deliver one of the Lectures in their Course, I feel myself in the path of duty, and therein I feel the elements of peace and quietness in the midst of much that is calculated to create distrust.

My subject is Priesthood. My object is twofold. First, Instruction in truth; and secondly, Defence against error. If no error existed, direct instruction in truth would be all that is required, as in the absence of disease wholesome food is all that a man stands in need of; but as in the presence of disease medicine is necessary as well as food, so in the presence of error controversy is indispensable, as well as instruction. Is controversy an evil? So is medicine. Is medicine, skilfully administered, beneficial? So is controversy. It is, indeed, possible to forget this remedial character of controversy, and to become fond of it for its own sake, as it is possible, however strange, for a student of anatomy to become enamoured of dissection. But it is also possible to endure controversy as an evil and to discharge it as a duty, while we sincerely grieve over it as a painful necessity. It is possible also, I hope, to conduct it with due regard to our own characters as Christians and gentlemen, and with due courtesy towards our opponents, however

A 2

seriously, or even fatally, mistaken we may conscientiously believe them to be.

Priesthood is a remedial institution. It presupposes the existence of evil to be remedied. If man had never fallen from God, this world would never have heard the sound of remedy, because it would never have felt the touch of disease. But, as it is, the whole history of the world, in every department, is a history of remedy. *Politically,* all laws, all forms of government, all constitutions, are remedies devised by the best wisdom of civilized and educated men to guard against what would otherwise be the unrestrained barbarism of human society. *Socially,* all relationships of life, beginning with the sanctity of the marriage contract, are remedies against what would otherwise be the mere animal herdings of brutalized man; and, *Religiously,* all applications of revealed truth, administered as they are by the hands of a competent and divinely-appointed Priest, are remedies ordained in the wisdom and goodness of God to guard against what would otherwise be the utterly ruinous condition of the whole human race.

We have said, and said it so often that it has become a proverb, that "prevention is better than cure." Now, in the most important subject of all Almighty God has not thought so. He has not acted so. His love towards mankind has not been manifested by prevention in the garden of Eden, but by cure in the garden of Gethsemane. In the exercise of a wisdom which is not to be fathomed by man's foolishness, He did not interpose to prevent the necessity of Priesthood; but He did interpose, by the appointment of a Priesthood, to meet the necessity.

A priest is a man appointed of God to do three things for other men—to teach them (the priest's lips should keep knowledge) to offer sacrifices for their sins, and to pray for their help and happiness. All these are remedial. If man had never fallen from God, there would have been no ignorance of God among men, and therefore no occasion for teaching; there would have been no sin against God, and therefore no occasion for sacrifice; no helplessness and misery, and therefore no occasion for intercession. Or had fallen man retained power to recover himself, to make satisfaction for his own sins to the Divine government, and to restore himself to the Divine image, there would have been no occasion for Priesthood; for then each individual would either have exercised the power within him and recovered and saved himself, or, neglecting to do so, would have continued alienated and lost for ever. Or had it pleased God to allow the fall of the first man to become irremediable for the whole race, there would have been no place for Priesthood. Thus we perceive that from the fallen and helpless condition of man on one side, and the redeeming mercy of God on the other, sprang the institution of Priesthood.

It was the purpose of Almighty God to make this institution perfect in His dear Son—the everlasting Son of the Father, co-equal and co-eternal, who in the beginning was with God, and was God. He was foreordained before the foundation of the world to take the manhood into God, and to be the perfect Teacher, the all-sufficient sacrifice, and the ever-living Intercessor. To Him men were to look for knowledge of God, to Him for pardon and merit, to Him for sympathy and peace, to Him for happiness and glory. True religion among men was in every instance to be a negotiation with God through Him—a truly divinely-appointed and altogether competent Priest—God and man in one Christ.

It was not the Divine purpose to send that Priest into the world immediately, when he was first required. Four thousand years of the history of a fallen world were to elapse before the foreordained Priest appeared. But during that time God did not leave Himself without witness. I speak not now of the witness of nature and conscience, under which some men did indeed make wonderful progress in civilization, and produced masterpieces of art, of eloquence, of poetry, of heroism. But, singular enough, and most significantly instructive, during all that time, whatever progress they made in other departments, they made none in the knowledge of God. In the wisdom of God, the world by wisdom knew not, and proved that they knew not, God.

They continued to worship the works of their own hands, and the most advanced amongst them had their highest altars inscribed to an unknown and unknowable idol. But there was a closer witness. It pleased God to select a people from the nations, and to educate them by a practice well calculated to accustom the human mind to the great cardinal, fundamental truth, that without the shedding of blood, which is the life—without inflicting death, which is the wages of sin—there could be no remission of sin. In order to teach them this, He was pleased to appoint priests, and to specify all the details of their peculiar duties.

The Jewish worshipper was taught that, however sincere and devout he might be, he could not transact his own business with God, he could not come direct to God, he must put his case into the hands of another, and that other was the priest; thus giving wonderful power, and place, and importance, to the man so employed. He stood betwen God and men. All the religious feelings and exercises of the people had reference to the priest. Every pang of conscious guilt drove the sinner to the priest, because only by the priest could the appointed sacrifice for guilt be offered. Every experience of sorrow, or want, or weakness drove the sufferer to the priest, because only by the priest could the acceptable intercession be made before the mercy-seat. Every deliverance from sickness or disease drove the grateful worshipper to the priest, because only by the priest could the freewill offering appointed be presented before God.

Judaism in all this was a shadow of good things then future. It was God's own primer, or first lesson-book, whereby He was teaching Christianity by object lessons. The measures with which the coming truth was seen through the existing shadow were very various in various individuals ; some resting in the shadow itself as in a formal act, and seeing little or nothing beyond; others penetrating through the shadow, and anticipating, with wonderful clearness, the eternal truth foreshadowed by the passing figure.

So matters stood until Jesus came. Then was a period of transition between Judaism and Christianity. During the ministry of Jesus upon earth the transition was going on. The Great Teacher was come, and was giving His Divine lessons; but the Great Sacrifice was not yet offered. The Great Intercessor had not yet entered into the true holy place. This will explain the treatment of the leper by our Lord and Saviour Jesus Christ. When the leper came to Him He did not simply desire him to go to the priest ; that would have been unmitigated Judaism. Neither did He cure him at once, and send him home, ignoring altogether the existence of a priest upon earth ; that would have been perfected Christianity. But it was a time of transition. Judaism was expiring indeed. The last sands were running out of its glass, but it was not yet actually superseded. Christianity was there, but had not entered into all its functions. Both were there, and the Lord's treatment partook of both. He cured the leper with a word, thereby showing that the Jewish priest, with all his ceremonies, was no longer required; still he was there. And Jesus recognised his office, saying, "Go, show yourself to the priest, and offer him the accustomed gift according to law," and this, He said, would be a testimony unto them. Now, we may very fitly ask, a testimony of what? Imagine the circumstances and cogitations of the priest when the man went to him. How comes this? Here is a man happily cured without our ceremonies, independent of us, and yet he acknowledges our office, and comes with a gift. It was a testimony of two things. First, that there was an individual in Israel who was independent of, and superior to all their ceremonies; and, secondly, that, although independent of them, He was friendly towards them, and willing to honour their great lawgiver. This was calculated to cause serious thoughts. There is a time for all things. There was a time for Judaism ; its time was rapidly expiring. Jesus, the great Teacher, became soon after the all-sufficient sacrifice, then rising from the dead, and passing into the heavens, He became the everlasting Intercessor. The shadows had passed away; the heavenly realities were come. " God took away the first, that he might establish the second." " There was verily a *disannulling* of the commandment going before, for the weakness and unprofitableness thereof."

There was a special difficulty in prevailing upon the Jews to admit that their priesthood had been temporary, and was now to be abolished. This difficulty arose partly from their knowledge that the priesthood in question was of Divine appointment originally, and that their forefathers had for centuries lived under it, worshipping the true God; and partly from the fact that the abuses which had crept into its exercise in the course of years had greatly contributed both to the pride of the priest, and to the indolence of the people.

The first controversy that Christianity had to wage with Judaism was with reference to the coming of Messiah. Was Messiah come? Was Jesus of Nazareth Messiah? This was the battle-ground on which the Apostles started, and with great power they give witness to the resurrection of the Lord Jesus, proving that this is very Christ. But that was not the only controversy they had; nor was it the controversy respecting which the Apostles wrote with the greatest care. There was another which may be called an inner controversy, not with Jewish unbelievers, but with Judaising professors of Christianity. The state of many of the Jews was described in the language addressed to St. Paul when he came to Jerusalem:—" Thou seest, brother, how many thousands of Jews there are which believe, and they are all zealous of the law." They were willing to receive Christianity provided they might have it in addition to Judaism, but they were not willing to have it instead of Judaism. It was this state of mind the Apostles had to combat. They had to show that the two things could not coexist; that the relation they bore to one another was not that of parts making up a whole, but that of type and antitype; the one in existence till the other came, and then vanishing away. Shall Judaism survive? Is there any place left for it? It is against this that some of the strongest arguments are directed in the Epistle to the Hebrews, and more especially in the Epistle to the Galatians. In that epistle the Apostle not only argues, but illustrates. He compares Judaism and Christianity to the two covenants, which were allegorized by the two wives of the patriarch Abraham. They could no more be made one religion than Hagar and Sarah could be made one woman; and their disciples could be no more united in one Church than Isaac and Ishmael could be made one child. The children of the bondwoman

are not to be, and never can be, heirs with the children of the free
woman. Having so argued, and so illustrated that point, the
Apostle exclaimed,—" Stand fast therefore in the liberty wherewith
Christ has made us free, and be not entangled again in the
yoke of bondage. Behold, I Paul say unto you, that if ye be
circumcised, Christ shall profit you nothing." Circumcision was
the initial rite of Judaism, *and is here put for the whole system.* If
you retain Judaism you cannot embrace Christianity. If you hold
to the priest that is on earth, you must relinquish the priest that
is in heaven.

. At the crisis of the abolition of Judaism and the introduction
of Christianity another answer had been given to this question,
although it was not perceived at the time. It had been given, not by
a voice, but by a hand from heaven. For remember this, every act
of Judaism, every detail of typical ritual, every sacrifice offered,
every lamp lighted, every incense burned, every attitude of the
celebrant priest, stood inseparably connected with the holy place
upon earth which was veiled from view by a curtain. Every act
outside was preparatory to the crowning act inside. The whole was
incomplete till the high priest went behind the veil. Take away
the veil the whole crumbled to pieces. There was neither form,
nor comeliness, nor meaning left in any part of it : and lo ! when
the true Priest offered the true sacrifice, when the Lord Jesus
bowed His head upon the cross, and gave up the ghost, behold
the veil of the temple was rent in twain from the top to the bottom
—I say it was God's own abolition of Judaism by a hand from
heaven.

Of this abolition the Jews had intimation in their own Scriptures, and for this they might have been prepared, had they duly
attended to the history of Abraham, and the language of David.
For, there, they would have learned that not any mortal man,
but a Priest from heaven, met the Patriarch and received his
homage : not any mortal man, for he was greater than Abraham
and blessed him, and there was not on the earth at the time a
greater man than Abraham : not any mortal man, for the Psalmist
declared concerning Him that he is a *Priest for ever.*

From all this, they might have known, as the Apostle afterwards taught, that a Priest was coming, not after the law of a
carnal commandment, but after the power of an endless life : the
true Melchisedec, the true Priest of the most High God, not made
without an oath and for a time, as was Aaron ; but with an oath
by him that said unto him, " The Lord sware and will not repent,
Thou art a Priest for ever after the order of the King of Righteousness."

. Is there, then, no priest upon earth ? In the sense of an offerer
for sin I am bold to say, none. That is, none of God's appoint-

ment. There are abundance of priests of man's invention or corrupt tradition. There are priests of Bhuddism, priests of Mahommedanism, priests of Romanism; I wish I could stop there. But the only priests of God's appointment upon earth were the priests of Judaism, and they were all merged in Him of whom it is written that He abideth a priest continually. They were not permitted to continue by reason of death; but this man because He continueth ever, hath an untransmissible priesthood.

And now Christianity is come, cleared of external things down to a very minimum. Not in the tabernacle, not in the temple, not on the mountains of Samaria, not in the city of Jerusalem are men now to worship, but everywhere. God is a Spirit. The hour was coming, and Jesus said it was then come, when they who worship the Father must worship Him in spirit and in truth. To the Samaritans he said, "Ye know not what ye worship." "Salvation," he said, "is of the Jews." They knew, or might have known—some of them did know what they worshipped, but there was no access to God except through the Jews. "Salvation was of the Jews." I pray you to study the words addressed to the Samaritan woman in the 4th chapter of the Gospel of St. John.

But in the face of all the spirituality so introduced, man's nature remains the same, and the natural man receiveth not the things of the Spirit of God. Now, if Christianity consists of the things of the Spirit of God, and if the natural man receives not the things of the Spirit of God, what is he to do with Christianity? He must either reject it altogether, or he must introduce into it things that are not things of the Spirit of God, and call them Christianity. This is what has been done. The great majority of those who professed Christianity from the beginning have been under the dominion of superstition, and superstition revels in external ceremonial. What else can it do? Stirred by its fears to take some action, and not having faith in the things that are not seen, what can it do but busy itself with the things that are seen? Therefore its priest must be visible, its confession must be addressed to something visible, its absolution must be pronounced by something visible. Instead of the hidden unction of the Holy One, it must have visible oil: instead of hidden godly sorrow, it must have visible penance. It walks by sight. This is not Christianity. This is a caricature of ancient Judaism, and like other caricatures it goes beyond its model in the way of excess. The Jewish priesthood offered sacrifices for the living, and for the living only. It remained for the exaggeration presented to the world by the great apostacy from the Christian faith to offer sacrifices not only for the living but for the dead.

You are aware that the point I have now reached has been

matter of controversy in this country for the last 300 years. But it has recently become a matter of more pressing urgency, because some of our own clergy claim all that the priests of the Church of Rome have ever claimed, and one of our own bishops—I am sorry to be obliged to say, but I must say it, because it is so—one of our own bishops has publicly declared that the English clergy are justified in believing that they have committed to them the same powers which the priests of the Catholic Church, both in the East and in the West, have ever *claimed* for their inheritance. This has made it a matter of such gravity as to demand interference— interference, if we are to be watchmen at all. This is one of the titles by which we are called in our ordination—"watchmen." What is a watchman for? To sleep while others sleep? To sleep while others wake? What is he good for? He is to be awake when others sleep, and he is to cry out when danger approaches, and make his voice heard. There is matter now for interference—I say, if we are to be watchmen at all—interference not by harsh language, not by calling opprobrious names without argument, as we have been slanderously reported, and as some affirm that we do. Where is the proof of it? I have been arguing for this half hour, and hope I have not used a single word that can deserve such a charge. And now, when I enter into the second branch of the subject, and come to the controversial, I hope still to refrain from saying a word that can be called per- sonally disrespectful of my brother clergymen. But I will not refrain from stating what I believe to be truth concerning the fatal heresies which are creeping into our Church.

I now approach the ground upon which such a claim to priesthood as I have described is advanced by some of the clergy of the English Church. They have a right, if we argue in this way against them, and invite a large assemblage of our fellow-citizens to hear us—they have a right that we should deal fairly with what they consider the strength of their position. I have no wish whatever to deal partially, or wilfully to avoid anything that would make for their claim. I cannot, indeed, make any large quotations from themselves. I would consider that a waste of your time, but I will endeavour to avoid any misrepresentation of what they have said.

The claim is grounded upon their interpretation of the language of Holy Scripture in the first place. First, upon the language addressed to St. Peter when our Lord said, "I will give unto thee the keys of the kingdom of heaven; and whatsoever thou shalt bind on earth, shall be bound in heaven; and whatsoever thou shalt loose on earth, shall be loosed in heaven"—words which He afterwards repeated to all His Apostles, "Whatsoever ye shall bind on earth shall be bound in heaven, and whatsoever ye shall loose on earth, shall be loosed in heaven." And once more upon the language which He addressed to ten of the twelve disciples in the evening of the day that He rose from the dead, when he said, " As my Father hath sent me, even so send I you. And when He had said this, He breathed on them, and said unto them, Receive ye the Holy Ghost: whose soever sins ye remit, they are remitted to them; and whose soever sins ye retain, they are retained."

These are solemn words; and if we refuse to receive the meaning attached to them by some of our brethren, we are bound, I think, in all fairness to give what we ourselves consider the meaning—not only to object, but, if we can, to instruct.

In the first place we observe that a parallel is here struck in ordinary language between the Lord's own mission and the mission then and there committed to His Apostles. " As my Father hath sent me, even so send I you." In considering this parallel discrimination is necessary, because, as you will soon perceive, it is not absolute,—it is not applicable in every point. The Father sent the Son to make an atonement by His own blood for the sins of the world. It has never been pretended on any side that the Son sent the Apostles to make an atonement by their blood for the sins of the world. Here there is no parallel. Again; the Father sent the Son to take human flesh, to carry it successfully and triumphantly through death to glory, without seeing corruption. It has never been pretended that the Son sent the Apostles likewise to carry human flesh through death triumphantly to glory. They died, and their sepulchres are with us to this day. Here there is no parallel. But in some points there must be a parallel, and an important one; and so there is. As the Father sent the Son to speak in His name and with His authority, so that whoever heard the Son heard Him, and whosoever believed the Son believed Him, and whosoever despised the Son despised Him,— even so the Son sent the Apostles to speak in His name. So He said to them—"He that heareth you heareth me; and he that despiseth you despiseth me; and he that despiseth me despiseth him that sent me."

Again, the Father sent the Son to work miracles, in attestation of the truth of His word. He declared Himself to be the true witness, testifying what He had seen; and in attestation of this claim He appealed to His works. " The works which the Father hath given me to finish, the same works that I do, bear witness of me that the Father hath sent me."

In like manner the Son sent the Apostles, and commissioned them to work miracles in attestation of their mission,—to heal the sick, cleanse the lepers, raise the dead. " Freely ye have received, freely give." And they did so. They went forth preaching everywhere, the Lord working with them, and confirming the word with signs following.

These are parallels. Thus, in the matter of making atonement there is no parallel: and in the matter of speaking the truth infallibly there is a parallel. It remains to be examined, whether in the matter of forgiving sins there is a parallel or not. It may be as exclusively the Son's work, as atonement was: or it may be as common to Him and His Apostles, as working miracles was. Which is the truth? Which did Jesus mean when He said, "Whose soever sins ye remit, they are remitted to them; and whose soever sins ye retain, they are retained."

What is the meaning of these words? Two interpretations are given to them. They are taken either to mean an application to the *persons* of men, conferring on the Apostles judicial powers to pardon or condemn; or to the *characters* of men in the light of God's revealed truth, conferring upon the Apostles infallible inspiration to declare what description of men are pardoned, and what description of men are condemned. I pray you to consider for a moment the first interpretation of these words. Taken in the first sense they invest the Apostles with absolute authority to loose or bind, to pardon or not to pardon, just as they pleased. There is no mention of the state of mind of the person, no allusion to his faith, to his opinions, to his character, or suffering. There is no restriction. The whole power is left unconditionally in the hands of the Apostles, as if THE LORD had said to them, Go ye into the world; be ye judges for eternity between man and man; whom you will, pardon; whom you will, condemn; salvation and damnation are in your hands. *You act as God.* "Whose soever sins ye remit, they are remitted; whose soever sins ye retain, they are retained." Now this is no caricature. This is taking the words as they are. Supposing this to be the literal meaning of the words, without paraphrase, without having recourse to any evasion, this, I say, is no caricature of the claim started by those who take this interpretation of the words. If it would not take me away from my immediate subject I could give an illustration of this,—that the claim put forth by the head of the great apostasy is in strict accordance with this view of the case. He has claimed authority over men and nations, and claims to be head over all states and kingdoms on the very plea that this is the meaning of these words. Those who claim less than this, and yet maintain this interpretation of the words, are obliged to introduce some paraphrase of modification. They do what they accuse us of doing. But we introduce no modification, as you will see.

The second interpretation of the words is that the Lord Jesus

Christ gave to the Apostles power and authority to state His truth so infallibly that their statements, in their application to every man upon earth, would be found in accordance with the decision of the God of heaven; as if Jesus had said to them, Go forth among men, teach my truth; you are in possession of the mind of God with regard to the salvation of men; when you declare on earth what description of men are pardoned, you are in strict accordance with the mind of God in heaven; when you declare on earth what description of men are condemned, again you are in strict accordance with the mind of God. *You speak as God.* It is in truth not you that speak, but the Holy Ghost that speaketh by you. This is no caricature on the other side. This is precisely what was claimed for the Apostles—that they had plenary inspiration. They spoke as God. I ask no paraphrase, but, taking this as the meaning of the words, I claim its absolute application to the men to whom it was addressed.

Now which of these is the true meaning of the words. This is the question to be tried, and how shall we try it? I propose to try it on five different issues.

1. First we inquire about the words themselves. Can we ascertain in any way whether the Jews were in the habit, in our Saviour's time, of using such words; if so, in what sense they used them? There is nothing in Holy Scripture to answer that; and therefore, in examining it, we must rely upon fallible testimony. But in an historical matter of this kind the testimony of man is ordinarily sufficient where there is no assignable reason why he should deceive. Now, it is on record that the Jews were in the habit of using such words as those, and I quote a passage from Lightfoot, in the third volume of his Commentary, where he says that binding and loosing in their vulgar speech signified to prohibit and to permit, or to teach what is prohibited or permitted, what lawful or unlawful:—

"Our wise men say that in Judah they did work on the Passover eve till noon, but in Galilee not at all, and as for the night, the school of Shammai *bound* it, that is, forbade to work in it, or taught that it was unlawful; but the school of Hillel *loosed* it till sunrising, or taught that it was lawful to work till sunrise.

"Rabbi Jochanan went from Tsipporis to Tiberias; he saith, 'Why brought ye to me this elder? for what I loose he binds, and what I bind he looseth.'

"'The Scribes have bound leaven,' that is, they have prohibited it. They have upon necessity loosed salutation on the Sabbath, *i.e.*, they have permitted it, or taught that it was lawful.

"Nachum asked Rabbi Jochanan concerning a certain matter, to whom he replied, 'Thou shalt neither bind nor loose.'

"Rabbi Chaiia said, 'Whatsoever I have bound to you elsewhere, I will loose to you here.' 'The mouth that bindeth is the mouth that looseth,' &c. Thousands of instances of this nature might be produced, by all which it is clear that the Jews' use of the phrase was of their doctors or learned men's *teaching* what was lawful and permitted, and what was unlawful and prohibited. Hence is that definition of such men's office and work :'A wise man, that judgeth judgment maketh unclean and maketh clean,'—'bindeth and looseth,' that is, teacheth what is clean and unclean, what is permitted and prohibited. And Maimonides, giving the relation of their ordaining of elders, and to what several employments they were ordained, said thus :—'A wise man that is fit to teach all the law, the consistory hath power to ordain him, to judge, but not to *teach*, *bound*, and *loose;* or power to teach, bound, and loose, but not to judge in pecuniary matters ; or power to both these, but not to judge in matters of mulct, &c.' So that the ordination of one to that function which was more properly ministerial, or to teach the people their duty—as what was lawful, what not ; what they were to do, what not to do, was to such a purpose, or in such a tenour as this, ' Take thou power to bind and loose, or to teach what is bound and loose,' for they use both expressions.

"By this vulgar and only sense of this phrase in the nation, the meaning of Christ using it there to His disciples is easily understood ; namely, that He first doth instate them in a ministerial capacity to teach, what bound and loose, what to be done and what not."

In claiming this then, as the meaning of the words, we are not putting any unprecedented, or extravagant, or unnatural meaning upon them ; and we are avoiding a meaning so unnatural, and a consequent claim so extravagant, that except by the Papacy in the plenitude of its arrogance, it has never been consistently acted on.

2. The next step in the inquiry is, can we ascertain what the Apostles themselves thought was the meaning of the words ? Is there anything in the manner in which they acted and spoke which throws light upon their own opinion of the nature of their commission ? Did they act and speak as men who felt themselves invested with judicial power over the persons of their fellow-men, or did they act and speak as men who felt that they had an infallible gift to teach what was true to their fellow-men ? Which would you say, from a knowledge of the Acts of the Apostles and the Epistles ? Which was their manner of treatment ?

(1.) Take the very first scene, when the Apostle Peter had the keys given to him to open the Gospel to the Jews. It was on the day of Pentecost he preached the Word, multitudes were pricked to the heart, and cried out, Men and brethren, what shall we do ? What did he say ? Did he address these sin-stricken creatures as a man possessing power to forgive sin ? There is no trace of it. What did he do, then ? He preached the Gospel—he proclaimed the salvation by Jesus Christ. He said, "Repent, and be baptized, every one of you, in the name of Jesus Christ, for the remission of sins, and ye shall receive the gift of the Holy Ghost." And when he used the other key, when by a vision from heaven he was directed to the house of a Gentile, and found Cornelius waiting for him, there was a case for exercising the full functions of his office. Here was the case of a sinner desiring to know the way of salvation according to the will of God. What then did the Apostle do? He did what we allege the Lord desired him. He proclaimed the truth. He preached Jesus, and said, "To him give all the prophets witness that, through His name, whosoever believeth in Him shall receive remission of sins." Now I ask any fair inquirer, is there any trace on these two occasions in the history of St. Peter—is there the slightest intimation of his having felt that he possessed what is now claimed as priestly power? He acted as if he possessed, what we claim from the words, infallible inspiration to tell the truth. He acted like a man who felt that. But if he felt that he had the other power, he strangely concealed it, and has left us no trace of it in his history. Some will say, Do you forget Ananias? is not that a trace? But what is it a trace of? Look at it. Ananias sold his possessions, and kept back part of the price, and laid down the other part as if it had been the whole, at the apostle's feet. Peter saw through the cheat. Exercising that gift of the Holy Ghost, the discernment of spirits, he saw what Ananias had done. And what did he do? He spoke to him. He spoke the truth. He said, "Ananias, why has Satan filled thine heart to lie to the Holy Ghost, and to keep back part of the price of the land? Thou hast not lied unto men, but unto God." Peter did not strike Ananias down. It was the finger of God that struck him down. All that Peter did was to speak. Here was no confession. Here was no refusal of absolution. Here was the detection of a hypocrite, followed by the immediate judgment from the Almighty.

Contrast this with Peter's conduct with reference to another part of his commission. I told you that our Lord said to the Apostles when they were to go forth they were to heal the sick, to cleanse the leper, to raise the dead, to work miracles. Well now, let us see how they understand that part of the commission. Peter and John found as they were going into the temple one afternoon a man that was lame from his mother's womb. The man, who was forty years of age, lay at the gate of the temple begging alms. When Peter and John were going past him he begged an alms, and Peter looking at him said—"Look on us." He looked, expecting to get something. Then Peter said—"Silver and gold have I none, but what I have I give unto thee." What I have! What had he? "In the name of Jesus Christ of Nazareth, rise and walk."

The power of working miracles he had in him. He committed himself before all, for he lifted the cripple by his hand, and immediately his feet and ankle bones received strength, and he leaped and walked, and praised God. Here then Peter acted as a man who knew he had the power to work miracles, but he never acted as a man who knew that he had the power to forgive sins.

(2.) And now look at the case of St. Paul. When the words under examination were addressed to the Apostles, Paul was not an Apostle. At that time he was a persecutor. When he was changed from being a persecutor, and made an Apostle, he received his commission from the same Divine source. Was the commission given to St. Paul identical in meaning with that which had been given to the other Apostles before, or was it diverse? If diverse, where is the unity of the commission—where is the unity of the Church? If identical, then we have in it the grand advantage of what may be called another version given by the Lord Himself, of the commission that He had given to the Apostles. If any of my Reverend Brethren who wholly disagree with us on this great question should happen to be in this meeting, I most earnestly and affectionately beg his attention, and ask him to look at the commission given to St. Paul. Here it is:

Jesus said to him, "Rise, and stand upon thy feet, for I have appeared unto thee for this purpose, to make thee a minister and a witness both of these things which thou hast seen, and of those things in which I will appear unto thee: delivering thee from the people, and from the Gentiles, unto whom now I send thee, to open their eyes, and to turn them from darkness to light, and from the power of Satan unto God, that they may receive forgiveness of sins, and inheritance amongst them which are sanctified by faith that is in me." And what interpretation did the Apostle put upon these words? How did he proceed to fulfil his commission? He said, "Whereupon, O King Agrippa, I was not disobedient unto the heavenly vision: but showed first unto them of Damascus, and at Jerusalem, and throughout all the coasts of Judea, and then to the Gentiles, that they should repent and turn to God, and do works meet for repentance." Thus, in proclaiming the truth he was doing what he understood himself to be desired to do. He was rendering what he himself considered obedience to the heavenly vision. Here is no mention of Priesthood, no figurative language which can be misconstrued into any meaning of Priesthood. Here is no mention of binding or loosing, retaining or remitting. On the contrary, all here corresponds with our interpretation of our Lord's words to the other Apostles. St. Paul was constituted a minister and a witness, but not a priest. If the two commissions be not identical in meaning, St. Paul's was grievously defective—

yet he was not behind the chiefest of the Apostles: if they be identical, there is nothing of Priesthood in either.

But, passing from the commission to the ministry of St. Paul, our opponents in this argument make much of his treatment of the incestuous Corinthian, as supplying an instance of that priestly authority to forgive sins, the existence of which we deny.

Now, my friends, I beg your attention to this case. It was a case of great scandal in the Church of Corinth. A professed believer in Christianity had been guilty of a sin which was abhorrent even to the natural conscience of the heathen. What were they to do with this man? The Apostle was absent. They wrote to him, asking his advice in the matter, inquiring what they were to do with this offender. He stated in reply what they were to do, and very strong was his language, commanding them to separate the offender from their company. His language was, " I verily, as absent in body, but present in spirit, have judged already, as though I were present, concerning him that hath so done this deed. In the name of our Lord Jesus Christ, when ye are gathered together, and my spirit, with the power of our Lord Jesus Christ, to deliver such an one unto Satan for the destruction of the flesh, that the spirit may be saved in the day of the Lord Jesus." And after a few words of warning, he winds up by saying, " Therefore *put away from among yourselves* that wicked person."

This separation from the Church was the punishment. The language will be explained if you bear in mind that the Apostle divided mankind into two classes—the Church and the world, and that he describes the world as governed by the devil. Satan he calls the god of this world, the prince of the power of the air. To cast a man out of the Church was to cast him back into the power of Satan; and this was the meaning of the language he used, "put away from among yourselves this wicked person." That was done. The punishment was inflicted by the Church upon the offender and penitence followed. A fresh perplexity then arose in the Church, as to what they were to do. Were they to receive him back, or was his offence to be considered irretrievable. Again the Apostle wrote, " Sufficient to such a man is this punishment, which was inflicted of many. So that contrariwise ye ought rather to forgive him, and comfort him, lest perhaps such a one should be swallowed up with overmuch sorrow. Wherefore I beseech you that ye would confirm your love towards him. For to this end also did I write, that I might know the proof of you, whether ye be obedient in all things. To whom ye forgive anything, I forgive also; for if I forgave anything, to whom I forgave it, for your sakes forgave I it in the person of Christ." As if the Apostle had said, You wrote to me when

B

he was an offender. I told you to put him away for his good. You have inflicted a punishment upon him—*inflicted by many*, not by me as a priest, but by the whole Church. That has brought him to his senses. And now he repents. And you ask what are you to do, O, receive him back, and forgive him. That there was nothing of auricular confession by St. Paul—that there was nothing of absolution by St. Paul—that there was nothing of what is commonly called priesthood in the case, is proved by the simple fact that the occurrence from first to last took place in the city of Corinth, and that Paul was in Macedonia. He wrote from Philippi.

I must further observe, under this head, that the Apostles never called themselves priests. Neither is this because they are altogether reticent concerning themselves and their office. St. Peter called himself an elder, St. John twice called himself the elder, and he describes his office as that of a herald. " That which we have seen and heard, declare we unto you, that ye also may have fellowship with us; and truly our fellowship is with the Father, and with his Son Jesus Christ." Here was the highest achievement of the glorious Gospel in the simplest way pronounced. " That which we have heard, declare we unto you, that ye also may have fellowship with us; and truly our fellowship is with the Father, and with his Son Jesus Christ." St. Paul describes his office as that of an ambassador for Christ, and he glories as the climax of the grace given to him in his privilege that he should be a preacher among the Gentiles of the unsearchable riches of Christ. But some one may remind me, Does not St. Paul call himself a steward of the mysteries of God? He does. " Let a man so account of us, as of the ministers of Christ, and stewards of the mysteries of God." And now, brethren, what are the mysteries of God of which the Apostle was a steward? There are six things which St. Paul calls mysteries. The first is the incarnation, the mystery of godliness, called also the mystery of God. The second is the great apostacy, the mystery of iniquity. The third is the union of Christ and his Church, the mystery of marriage, which is a great mystery. The fourth is the union of the Jew and the Gentile in one body, a mystery concealed for ages and generations, but now made known, that the Gentiles should be fellow-heirs and of the same body. The fifth is the mystery of the final restoration of the Jews. " I would not, brethren, that ye should be ignorant of this mystery, lest ye should be wise in your own conceits; that blindness in part is happened to Israel; until the fulness of the Gentiles be come in. And so all Israel shall be saved." The sixth is the resurrection of the body. " Behold, I show you a mystery. We shall not all sleep, but we shall all be changed." To these six things the Apostle applies the word "mystery"; and it deserves your careful attention and your constant remembrance that the word "mystery" is never once in the Bible applied to either Baptism or the Lord's Supper. Outward and visible signs were designed to simplify, not to mystify; to explain, not to conceal, inward and spiritual realities.

I said that in no instance recorded in the New Testament does any one of the Apostles call himself a priest. If they had such an office as that which is now claimed for them, and for others through them, they were either negligent or culpably modest in hiding their divine claim. This is a case in which an argument may be legitimately based on silence; for had their priesthood been their special boast and glory—had it been the special characteristic of their mission, on which they laid the greatest stress —it is absolutely incredible, because it is morally impossible, that none of them should ever have made mention of it, as exercised either by himself or by any of his colleagues. Is it not incredible? Would it not be morally impossible for the reverend brethren to whom I have alluded very respectfully, and, I hope, without giving them any offence,—would it not be morally impossible for them to give up the pride of what is exultingly called catholic truth, and speak of themselves as ministers of Christ Jesus, without the slightest reference to priesthood? They could not do it. But this is made the more remarkable because one of the Apostles, in appointing successors to himself in the Christian ministry by laying on of hands and prayer, and giving them instructions how to behave themselves in the house of God,—the Church, the pillar and ground of the truth, has entirely forgotten the chiefest of all their functions, so as not to make the least allusion to it. He charges them to give attention to reading, to exhortation, to preach the Word, to be instant in season and out of season, to reprove, rebuke, exhort with all long-suffering and doctrine, to do the work of evangelists; to make full proof of their ministry. But there is not a word about priesthood. Alas! alas! for Timothy and Titus. With how small a measure of catholic truth were they entrusted! There was no priesthood in their case. No; but there was the preaching of the grace of God, through the true and only true Priest, Jesus Christ.

On these grounds we feel justified in maintaining that the meaning of our Lord's commission to the Apostles was, not that they were to be judges to deal with persons, and forgive or condemn, but that they were to be infallible teachers of truth, declaring who are forgiven and who are not forgiven, binding faith and salvation together on earth, and loosing unbelief from salvation on earth as God has done in heaven. The claim, then, which the priests of the Church of Rome make, to which I have already alluded, and which some of our brethren make, not only is a claim which the Apostles did not make,—not only did they not practise it,—but they did practise that which was inconsistent with it. There is no trace of it in the history of the Primitive Church. There is no allusion to it in the early councils of the Church. It was the offspring of sacerdotal pride and arrogance, put forth in the dark ages. England fought against it long, and at last threw it off. Is it now to be introduced amongst us?

3. In opposition to the claim, I urge, in the third place, the fact that there is a total absence from the New Testament of any sacrifice for sin to be offered by a priest.

If any man be a priest, it is of necessity that he have some sacrifice to offer. If any man have a sacrifice to offer, it is of necessity that with reference thereto and in that respect he is a priest. All Christians have sacrifices to offer,—spiritual sacrifices, acceptable to God through Jesus Christ. Therefore, in that respect, and with reference thereto, all Christians are priests. To this agrees the language of St. Peter, addressed to the Church dispersed, the strangers scattered throughout Pontus, Galatia, Cappadocia, Asia, and Bithynia. He calls them "an holy priesthood, to offer up spiritual sacrifices, acceptable to God by Jesus Christ." But observe, none of these are sacrifices *for sin*. They are sacrifices of love, of zeal, of self-denial, of gratitude; but they are in no sense or degree sacrifices for sin. For what is a sacrifice for sin? Sin is the transgression of God's law. A sacrifice for sin is an endurer of the death which sin deserves, substituted for the offender, who himself deserved the death. The only satisfying sacrifice for sin is Christ Himself, who offered Himself, pouring out His soul unto death, even the death of the cross. That was perfect. "There remains no more offering for sin." In opposition to this it is alleged that the priests of the New Testament offer Christ Himself in what is called the eucharistic sacrifice,—Christ objectively present in the consecrated elements. That is called in the Church of Rome an unbloody sacrifice. But an unbloody sacrifice for sin is a contradiction in terms, because the wages of sin is death. The blood is the life. The shedding of blood is the death; without shedding of blood there is no death, and without death there is no sacrifice for sin. It is vain to attempt to retain the reality of sacrifice, and at the same time to deny the reality of death. The language of the Church of Rome betrays this. The word used to describe the act of offering is *immolare*—to immolate or kill; and the word used to describe the thing offered is *hostia*—the victim. They declare that Christ is immolated in the Mass, and they hold up for adoration Christ the victim—*hostia*. Now let me ask our brethren who have expressed a longing for union with Rome, do they immolate Christ in the eucharistic sacrifice, and do they hold Him up as a victim for adoration? Many of you have read the "Church and the World." In that publication, in a paper by Mr. Medd, I find this:—

"As the most holy body and blood of Christ, the alone acceptable victim to make our peace with God, are *offered, that is* continually *presented and pleaded*, by Jesus Himself in heaven, naturally, as we may say, and openly; so the same most holy body and blood are continually presented and pleaded before God by Christ's representatives, acting in His name, and by His authority and commission upon earth."

In this passage "offered" is used as synonymous with presented and pleaded. If this be correct why should the Apostle say, "there remaineth no more offering for sin," seeing he never says there remaineth no more pleading for sin. Just the reverse. To plead is to pray. To offer *for sin* is to kill. I venture to repeat, It is vain to attempt to retain the reality of sacrifice for sin, and to deny the reality of death. And if any assert, as the Church of Rome does,* the reality of death in the Supper of the Lord, our answer is in the language of St. Paul:—"Christ being raised from the dead, *dieth no more:* death hath no more dominion over him. For in that he died, he died unto sin once: but in that he liveth, he liveth unto God." Who are they, then, that would put him to death again? Who are they that would crucify the Son of God afresh, immolate Him in the Mass, and hold Him up for adoration as a victim? Who but they who don't believe in His one offering, once offered, and in its all-sufficiency; they who have not faith to trust what God has done once for all, but must be perpetually doing, doing, doing something.

4. I resist their claim of priesthood, fourthly, because of the absence from the New Testament of any detailed instruction for the exercise of priesthood. This is made the more remarkable by contrast with the Jewish type. The Jewish priest had minutely detailed instructions concerning the leprosy, the great typical disease in its various phases; how to deal with it in every case;

---

* The words of the Council of Trent are these:—"Nam celebrato veteri pascha, quod in memoriam exitûs de Ægypto multitudo filiorum Israel *immolabat*, novum instituit Pascha se ipsum, ab Ecclesiâ per sacerdotes sub signis visibilibus *immolandum* in memoriam transitûs sui ex hôc mundo ad Patrem, quando per sui sanguinis effusionem nos redemit, eripuitque de potestate tenebrarum, et in regnum suum transtulit."

And again, in the next chapter,—"Et quoniam in divino hôc sacrificio, quod in Missâ peragitur, Idem ille Christus continetur, et incruente *immolatur*, qui in arâ Crucis semel se ipsum cruente obtulit," &c.

how, when, and under what circumstances they were to pronounce a man clean ; when, and under what circumstances they were to pronounce him unclean; when they were to shut him up for a week, and to examine him at the end of seven days, and then to pronounce upon him ; when they were to repeat the process for seven days more. All this you will find detailed in the 13th chapter of the Book of Leviticus. There all the particulars are mentioned, and I will give you a specimen of them :—" When a man shall have in the skin of his flesh a rising, a scab, or bright spot, and it be in the skin of his flesh like the plague of leprosy, then he shall be brought unto Aaron the priest, or to one of his sons the priest: and the priest shall look on the plague in the skin of the flesh : and when the hair in the plague is turned white, and the plague in sight be deeper than the skin of his flesh, it is a plague of leprosy : and the priest shall look on him and pronounce him unclean. If the bright spot be white in the skin of his flesh, and in sight be not deeper than the skin, and the hair thereof be not turned white, then the priest shall shut up him that hath the plague seven days : and the priest shall look on him the seventh day : and, behold, if the plague in his sight be at a stay, and the plague spread not in the skin, then the priest shall shut him up seven days more." I need not read further. All these symptoms were outward and visible. Any man, with the ordinary perception of a man, and with good eyesight was competent to deal with the circumstances of the case. All this was a type, as the priest himself was a type. But look at the anti-type. The seat of sin, the great leprosy of human nature, is the heart. There, within, is the deceitfulness and desperate wickedness. Hear His description, who would not exaggerate, and could not be deceived :—" From within, out of the heart of men, proceed evil thoughts, adulteries, fornications, murders, thefts, covetousness, an evil eye, blasphemy, pride, foolishness." With comparatively few exceptions, the workings of this great epidemic are not visible by man. No man can take cognisance of them ; no man can deal with them. The New Testament contains no directions concerning the various phases of sin, such as the Old Testament contains concerning the leprosy. And why so? Because the priesthood of the New Testament is not transferable from the Lord Jesus himself, and He requires no instructions. He sees the inward disease in all its subtle workings, as clearly as the typical priest saw the varying symptoms of the cutaneous eruption. He knows when to reprove, and when to encourage; when to wound, and when to heal; when to prolong mourning and heaviness, and when to pour in the oil of joy and gladness.

But if any of his ministers attempt to do this, where are their instructions? If any of our young clergymen, following the example of Dr. Pusey, and encouraged by what he has recently written, undertake to deal judicially with sin, and to apportion penance, are they presumptuous enough to suppose that they can do so impromptu, without any training or instruction? And where are they to procure this? Thank God there is no English literature on the subject. They must have recourse to the casuists of the Church of Rome, of whom it is no more than justice to say that they have thoroughly exhausted a disgusting subject. Of *Vasques, Viva, Cajetan, Dens, Liguori,* and others, it may be truly said that evil communications corrupt good manners. Their dissertations on the commandments, their sliding-scale of sin, their doubts expressed and solved, their probabilities advanced and retracted, their balancings apologetic of dishonesty, and suggestive of indecency, their proficiency in both the arts ascribed to the celebrated Roman conspirator, *simulatio et dissimulatio,* all these resemble the training of fiends for the destruction of men's souls, and not the thoughts, and principles, and practice of a priesthood established by the Lord Jesus Christ.

Much of what I have referred to has hitherto been kept in the monkish Latin in which it was originally written; but the time may come when it will become our bounden, though painful duty to rouse the indignation of Englishmen at the expense of their modesty, by translating and circulating some of the contents of that charnel-house.

5. I have but one clause more. We reject the claim to Priest-hood, fifthly, by an appeal to the language of the Church of England concerning confession and absolution. The word *priest,* as used in our Prayer-book, is an abbreviation of presbyter, which means an elder. In proof of this, I refer to the Latin version of our Thirty-nine Articles, where the word presbyter is used, and not *sacerdos,* which would have been the word had the person spoken of been designated a sacrificing priest. I refer also to the Thirty-second Canon, which is entitled, " None to be made deacon and *minister* both in one day." In this Canon the words minister and priest are used interchangeably.

The action of the minister or priest is distinctly referred to four times in our Book of Common Prayer.

(1) The first, in our daily service, defines with precision the " power and commandment " which God has given to His ministers. It is to *declare* and *pronounce* to His people, being penitent, the absolution and remission of their sins. The prerogative of *conferring* what the minister thus declares belongs to God alone. " HE pardoneth and absolveth all them that truly repent and unfeignedly believe His holy Gospel." Here every thing is in its

scriptural place. The donor of the blessing is God. The receiver of the blessing is the penitent believer. The messenger authorized to declare and pronounce the consolatory truth is the minister. The declaration itself is a transcript of the language which apostles spoke as they were moved by the Holy Ghost; and, therefore, in making this declaration every minister is actually binding on earth what is bound in heaven.

(2) The form of absolution in our Communion Service implies, without directly asserting, the ministerial office. It declares that Almighty God has promised forgiveness of sins to all them that with hearty repentance and true faith turn to Him, and then uses this animating and encouraging truth as the basis of a prayer that He may be pleased to do as He has said.

(3) The invitation to the Communion.

Introductory to this, let me remind you that St. Paul, writing on the subject of the Lord's Supper, says, " Let a man examine himself, and so let him eat of that bread, and drink of that cup." More generally, he says, " Examine your own selves, prove your own selves whether ye be in the faith." And St. John says, " If our heart condemn us, God is greater than our heart, and knoweth all things; if our heart condemn us not, then have we confidence towards God." From these and such portions of the Word of God it appears that every sincerely inquiring Christian may ascertain whether he is in the faith or not. Our Church, in her Catechism, asks, " What is required of them who come to the Lord's Supper ? " and answers, " To examine themselves," &c. And in this invitation, after plain and practical instructions for self-examination, she adds, " And because it is requisite that no man should come to the Holy Communion but with a full trust in God's mercy, and with a quiet conscience, therefore if there be any of you who by this means cannot quiet his own conscience herein, but requireth further comfort or counsel, let him come to me, or to some other discreet and learned minister of God's Word, and open his grief; that, by the ministry of God's Holy Word, he may receive the benefit of absolution, together with ghostly counsel and advice, to the quieting of his conscience, and avoiding of all scruple and doubtfulness."

We suppose the inquirer honest and sincere, and then we ask, Concerning what is it possible for such a man to have any real scruple or doubtfulness, and therefore to require any counsel or advice ? Not, surely, concerning any actual sin, such as he can confess as a sin. Not, surely, concerning any thing which he can to himself or to another truly call a sin. With reference to all such he knows his duty without any doubtfulness, whatever reluctance he may feel to forsake his sin. This is broadly stated in the preceding part of the invitation. With reference to known sin, such as he can confess, he can have no doubtfulness, and can require no counsel to remove embarrassing scruples. And therefore the interview with his minister to which he is here invited has no reference to known sins.

Concerning what then is it that he can really require counsel and advice, and the experienced ministry of God's Holy Word ?

We can readily understand that a man of a tender and scrupulous conscience may be in much perplexity concerning himself as in the presence of his God. He is conscious of certain motives of action, and he is doubtful whether they are Christian motives, or even compatible with real Christian sincerity. He feels the intrusion of thoughts which disturb him—sceptical thoughts, blasphemous thoughts, vain, self-sufficient thoughts, and he doubts whether they can co-exist with genuine saving Christianity. He may be in the state of mind described in one of our popular hymns—

> " 'Tis a point I long to know,
>   Oft it causes anxious thought,—
> Do I love the Lord or no—
>   Am I His, or am I not ? "

In this state of mind, and with possibly a very limited acquaintance with the Word of God, he may not be able to avoid scruples and doubtfulness, and attain to a full confidence in God's mercy, and a quiet conscience. And because it is requisite that, without such confidence and quiet, he should not come to the Holy Communion, he is invited to take counsel with some minister of God's Word, whose more extensive acquaintance with the contents of Holy Scripture may meet his scruples, solve his doubts, and so " by the ministry of God's Holy Word he may receive the benefit of absolution, together with ghostly counsel and advice, to the quieting of his conscience."

This is the sort of case contemplated in the invitation.

The occasion is expressly limited to preparation for the Communion. It is his *grief herein*, and not his griefs in the plural number, as Dr. Pusey writes it, that he is to open. The help given is limited to the ministry of God's Holy Word. The whole absolutely excludes any confession of known sin, or any habitual resort to the minister for that purpose.

(4) The only remaining passage is in the Service for the Visitation of the Sick.

The language here is more pointed, because it is more personal. The minister is no longer dealing with general declarations, to be appropriated or not, according to the various characters of those who hear him. All that belongs to *character* has been already investi-

C

gated, as far as man can investigate the mind of his fellow-man. Having received from the sick man, satisfactory answers as to his repentance and faith, the minister is thus directed :—" Here shall the sick person be moved to make a special confession of his sins, if he feel his conscience troubled with any weighty matter. After which confession the priest shall absolve him (if he humbly and heartily desire it) after this sort. Our Lord Jesus Christ, who hath left power to His Church to absolve all sinners who truly repent and believe in Him, of His great mercy forgive thee thine offences. And by His authority committed to me, I absolve thee from all thy sins, in the name of the Father, and of the Son, and of the Holy Ghost. Amen." Then follows this prayer for the forgiveness of this very person :—" O, most merciful God, who, according to the multitude of thy mercies, dost so put away the sins of those who truly repent, that thou rememberest them no more, open thine eye of mercy upon this thy servant, *who most earnestly desireth pardon and forgiveness.*" I need read no more.

On this, I observe, first, that there is no intimation in the Service of the sick person being alone with the minister. On the contrary, the responses in the Service in praying for the sick involve the necessity of others being present. This excludes, *in limine*, all auricular confession. That is the first step.

Secondly, if the words be a declaration of God's pardon to the penitent they are in harmony with the prayer that follows imploring such pardon. But if they be a description of an act of pardon then and there performed by the minister actually clearing the sinner from his sins, the prayer that follows is superfluous, unsuitable, out of place—it is a work of supererogation. But as a further argument to show what reason we have for believing that the words were intended as a declaratory statement of God's forgiveness of the penitent and not an act of the minister at the moment, I refer to the Canons of the Church of 1603. They have not the force of law, with the exception of one which is embodied in the Act of Uniformity: but they have all the force of Convocation when acting under the Royal License. In the 45th and 46th of these Canons the difference is clearly laid down between incumbents that were preachers and incumbents that were not preachers. At that time a large number of men became ministers of a preaching Church, but that did not qualify them as preachers, and they could not preach. To meet this necessity a book of Homilies was prepared, and they were desired to read them. But there were some incumbents who were competent to preach and licensed as preachers, and the distinction between them and the non-preachers is made clear, and is defined in the Canons which I have referred to. In the 67th Canon we read these words :—" When any person is dangerously sick in any parish, the minister or curate, having knowledge thereof, shall resort unto him or her (if the disease be not known or probably suspected to be infectious) to instruct and comfort them in their desires, according to the order of the Communion-book, *if he be no preacher;* or, *if he be a preacher, then as he shall think most needful and convenient.*"

If the man was no preacher—if he was incompetent to declare the Gospel, he had words provided for him by the Church that he was to use, more likely to proclaim God's mercy than any stammerings of his own. But if he was a preacher—if he knew how to proclaim the grace of God in Christ, then he was not to use the words, except he thought them fit, but words that he thought most fit and expedient. Does this not plainly imply that in the mind of Convocation the meaning of the passage was preaching the Gospel ? The use of the words was prescribed to non-preachers. But preachers were at liberty to use other words as they saw fit. Under this Canon, none of us are now bound to use these words. If any man ask me to use that service, my answer is, " No ! I can preach," and am therefore commissioned by the Church to use such words as I think most needful and convenient —these, or others to the same purpose.

If any of my brethren in the ministry, having regard to the Canon of the Church, feel themselves *compelled* to use the *ipsissima verba* of this service, I can only condole with them, on the confession thereby made, that they are not preachers, and therefore not competent, and therefore not at liberty, to use such words as they shall think most needful and convenient.

Well, dear friends, I must now conclude. I look up, I look up to our Great High Priest ; of the things we have spoken this is the sum. We have such a High Priest, who is at the right hand of the throne of the Majesty of heaven, touched with a feeling of our infirmities. There He sits in the glorious Confessional, and this whole earth is but one of the whispering galleries of His great temple of the universe. Whisper, and it reaches His ear, it reaches His heart. He has every qualification, His sympathies are perfect, because He has human nature without any mixture of human selfishness. It is selfishness that mars sympathy. In proportion as selfishness prevails sympathy is dulled. In Jesus there is no selfishness. There is all perfect sympathy. Imagine a vessel wrecked in deep water, near to a rock, and there is a man on the rock. The struggling creatures thrown at once into the water, cry for help. To whom do they cry ? Not to one another. They are all in like circumstances, and cannot help one another. Not to the rock. It has no feeling for them. To whom then do they cry ? To the man on the rock. He is of their nature, and can feel for them. He is not in their circumstances, and can help them. Christ is the man on the rock. Cry to Him in your trouble. Lift up your hearts to Him. Make known your desires to Him. O beware how you open heart or soul to a fellow-sinner. You may, for mutual benefit, confess your faults one to another, that you may pray for one another. In the confidence of Christian friendship you may entrust a secret, that your friend may help you to pray for God's blessing. But that is the *mutual* confidence of friendship, and has nothing in it of the prostration of priesthood. Keep clear of the Confessional upon earth. If it ever prevail again in England farewell to domestic happiness, farewell to domestic peace, farewell to mutual trust and confidence between parent and child—aye, between husband and wife. England, have done with it. Our forefathers discarded it. In the name of God, never receive it again.

www.ingramcontent.com/pod-product-compliance
Lightning Source LLC
Chambersburg PA
CBHW022041080426
42733CB00007B/933